ALGEBRA MAKES SENSE

Interactive Tasks for Algebra Learners

Using Equations to Solve Problems

Murray Britt

Peter Hughes

Randall Souviney

Dale Seymour Publications®

Parsippany, New Jersey

Project Editor: Jane Books
Editorial Manager: Carolyn Coyle
Production/Manufacturing Director: Janet Yearian
Production/Manufacturing Manager: Karen Edmonds
Production/Manufacturing Coordinator: Jennifer Murphy
Art Director: Jim O'Shea
Text and Cover Design: Robert Dobaczewski

Dale Seymour Publications
An imprint of Pearson Learning
299 Jefferson Road, P.O. Box 480
Parsippany, New Jersey 07054-0480
www.pearsonlearning.com
1-800-321-3106

ISBN 0-7690-2838-1

1 2 3 4 5 6 7 8 9 10-MZ-04 03 02 01

Dear Algebra Student,

Have you ever wondered if algebra is useful in the real world? People have been using algebra to solve problems for over 1,000 years. In this book you will learn how to write equations to represent problems and how to use these equations to solve the problems.

To help you become skillful in using equations for solving problems, you will work with *arithmagons*. What's an arithmagon? Just look at the diagrams below. Pairs of circle numbers in an arithmagon must always add up to the values in the connected squares. In this book, you will see how algebra can be a powerful tool for finding the missing circle numbers for any arithmagon.

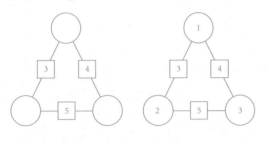

You will also learn how you can use algebra to prove mathematical conjectures. For example, one way to calculate the sum of the three consecutive numbers 4, 5, and 6 is to multiply the middle number by 3 ($4 + 5 + 6 = 3 \times 5 = 15$). Using algebra, you can prove the conjecture that multiplying the middle number of any three consecutive numbers by 3 will always give you the sum of the three numbers.

You will notice Practice Plus icons like this as you work through the book.

Page 48

These icons identify key ideas and skills that you will need to know in order to study algebra successfully. Sometimes you may find that you still need more practice on some skills. If so, turn to the Practice Plus and Cumulative Practice pages at the end of the book for additional practice.

We hope that as you complete the investigations in this book, you will learn how to construct and use equations to solve problems.

Good luck,
Murray Britt
Peter Hughes
Randall Souviney

Contents

Investigating Word Problems

Task A

Larry wants to solve this problem.

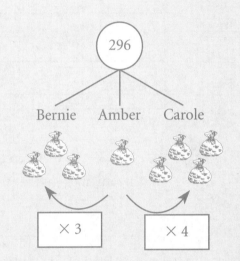

> Amber, Bernie, and Carole share 296 marbles. Bernie gets 3 times as many as Amber, and Carole gets 4 times as many as Amber. How many marbles does each person get?

Larry begins by drawing this diagram to represent the problem. He draws 1 bag of marbles for Amber, 3 bags for Bernie, and 4 bags for Carole.

1 Explain why Larry might represent the amounts of marbles for Amber, Bernie, and Carole in this way.

2 Larry claims that there are 296 ÷ 8 = 37 marbles in each bag. Decide whether Larry is correct, and explain your thinking.

③ Complete this table, using the diagram in Task Box A to help you. Show your calculations.

Name	Number of Marbles
Amber	37
Bernie	
Carole	

④ Larry draws this diagram to solve another word problem. Fill in the three missing numbers in the problem below.

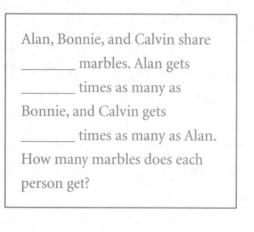

Alan, Bonnie, and Calvin share _____ marbles. Alan gets _____ times as many as Bonnie, and Calvin gets _____ times as many as Alan. How many marbles does each person get?

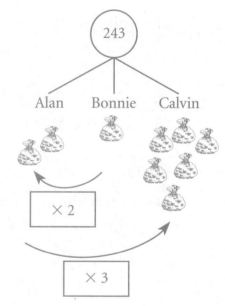

⑤ Complete the following sentence and show your calculation.

The number of marbles in each bag is _____.

Now complete this table, using Larry's diagram to help you. Show your calculations.

Name	Number of Marbles
Alan	
Bonnie	
Calvin	

 You can use this diagram to help you solve this problem. Fill in the circle and boxes in the diagram.

Alan, Bonnie, and Calvin share 477 marbles. Alan gets 3 times as many as Bonnie, and Calvin gets 5 times as many as Bonnie. How many marbles does each person get?

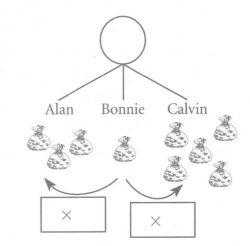

 Complete the following sentence. Show your calculation.

The number of marbles in each bag is _____.

9   Complete the table. Show your calculations.

Name	Number of Marbles
Alan	
Bonnie	
Calvin	

10 Think about how you could solve this problem.

Alan, Bonnie, and Calvin share 351 marbles. Alan gets 3 times as many as Bonnie, and Calvin gets 3 times as many as Alan. How many marbles does each person get?

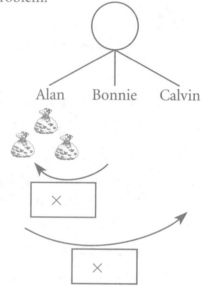

a. Draw the bags of marbles for Bonnie and Calvin. Then fill in the circle and boxes in the diagram.

b. Complete the table. Show your work.

Name	Number of Marbles
Alan	
Bonnie	
Calvin	

Algebra Makes Sense

11 Read the problem below. A diagram has been started to help you solve it.

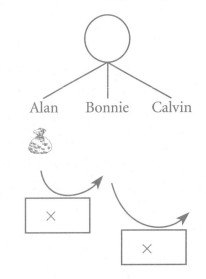

Alan, Bonnie, and Calvin share 310 marbles. Bonnie gets 3 times as many as Alan, and Calvin gets 2 times as many as Bonnie. How many marbles does each person get?

a. Draw the bags of marbles for Bonnie and Calvin. Then fill in the circle and boxes in the diagram.

b. Complete the table. Show your calculations.

Name	Number of Marbles
Alan	
Bonnie	
Calvin	

To solve the problem below, you will need to work backwards.

Alan, Bonnie, and Calvin share 423 marbles. Calvin gets 6 times as many as Alan and 3 times as many as Bonnie. How many marbles does each person get?

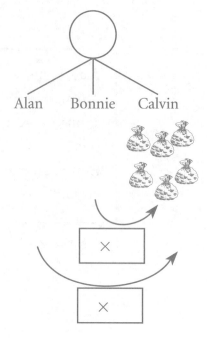

 Draw the bags of marbles for Alan and Bonnie. Then fill in the circle and boxes in the diagram.

b. Complete the table. Show your calculations.

Name	Number of Marbles
Alan	
Bonnie	
Calvin	

What you have learned so far can help you solve this problem.

Alan, Bonnie, and Calvin share 392 marbles. Alan gets 4 times as many as Calvin and 2 times as many as Bonnie. How many marbles does each person get?

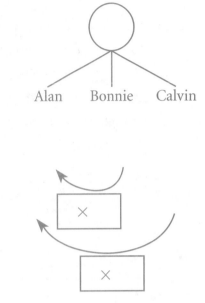

a. Draw the bags of marbles for Alan, Bonnie, and Calvin. Then fill in the circle and boxes in the diagram.

b. Complete the table. Show your calculations.

Name	Number of Marbles
Alan	
Bonnie	
Calvin	

Larry's friend Serena says that she can use this diagram to help her figure out that Alan gets 60 marbles. Study the diagram. Notice that Bonnie has 1 bag plus 3 marbles and Calvin has 1 bag plus 2 marbles.

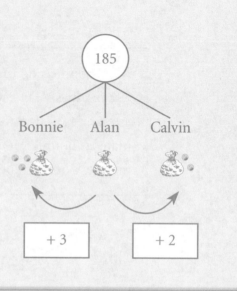

 14 Decide whether Serena is correct and explain why or why not.

 15 Complete the following table. Show your calculations for Bonnie and Calvin.

Name	Number of Marbles
Alan	
Bonnie	
Calvin	

16 Write a word problem that Serena has solved.

Think about how you could solve this problem.

Alan, Bonnie, and Calvin share 211 marbles. Bonnie gets 2 times as many as Alan, and Calvin gets 6 more than Bonnie. How many marbles does each person get?

a. Complete the diagram above for Alan, Bonnie, and Calvin, using bags and dots to represent their marbles.

b. Complete the table. Show your calculations.

Name	Number of Marbles
Alan	
Bonnie	
Calvin	

 Serena begins this diagram to solve the problem below. Serena says that Calvin must get 2 more marbles than Alan. Explain why this is true.

Alan, Bonnie, and Calvin share 261 marbles. Alan gets 3 times as many as Bonnie and 2 fewer than Calvin. How many marbles does each person get?

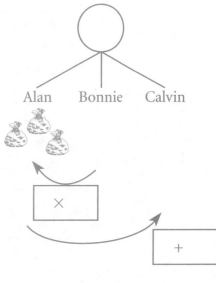

Complete Serena's diagram on page 13.

 Now complete the table and show your calculations.

Name	Number of Marbles
Alan	
Bonnie	
Calvin	

 A diagram has been started for the problem below.

Alan, Bonnie, and Calvin share 290 marbles. Alan gets half as many as Bonnie, who gets 5 fewer than Calvin. How many marbles does each person get?

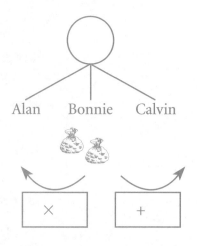

a. Complete this diagram for Alan, Bonnie, and Calvin.

b. Now complete the table, showing your calculations.

Name	Number of Marbles
Alan	
Bonnie	
Calvin	

Kareem begins a diagram for this problem.

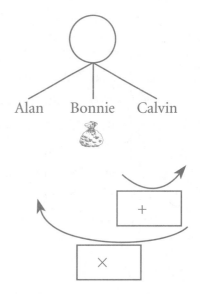

Alan, Bonnie, and Calvin share 513 marbles. Calvin gets 3 more than Bonnie, and Alan gets 2 times as many as Calvin. How many marbles does each person get?

a. Complete the diagram.

b. Now complete the table and show your calculations.

Name	Number of Marbles
Alan	
Bonnie	
Calvin	

Use what you have learned so far to decide how to represent this problem.

Alan, Bonnie, and Calvin share 302 marbles. Bonnie gets $\frac{2}{3}$ of what Alan gets. Calvin gets 5 more than twice what Alan gets. How many marbles does each person get?

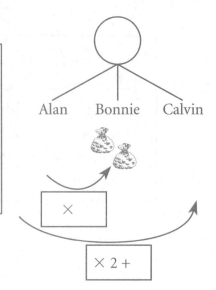

a. Complete this diagram for Alan, Bonnie, and Calvin.

b. Calculate the number of marbles in 1 bag. Show your work.

c. Now complete the table below. Show your calculations.

Name	Number of Marbles
Alan	
Bonnie	
Calvin	

Reggie looks at the problem below and wonders who has the least number of marbles. Think about how you can solve this problem.

> Alan, Bonnie, and Calvin share 402 marbles. Bonnie gets 3 times as many as Alan, and Alan gets $\frac{1}{2}$ as many as Calvin. How many marbles does each person get?

 Complete this diagram for Alan, Bonnie, and Calvin.

Alan   Bonnie   Calvin

 Calculate the number of marbles in 1 bag. Show your calculations.

26 Now complete the table. Show your calculations.

Name	Number of Marbles
Alan	
Bonnie	
Calvin	

Think about how you can solve this problem. Complete the diagram.

Alan, Bonnie, and Calvin share 423 marbles. Alan gets 3 fewer than Calvin, and Bonnie gets 3 times as many as Alan. How many marbles does each person get?

Alan   Bonnie   Calvin

 Calculate the number of marbles in 1 bag. Show your calculations.

29 Now complete the table. Show your calculations.

Name	Number of Marbles
Alan	
Bonnie	
Calvin	

Practice PLUS 1
Page 48

Algebra Makes Sense

Investigating How to Use Equations to Solve Problems

Task A

Larry and Serena each work on solving the following problem.

> Alan, Bonnie, and Calvin share 153 marbles. Alan gets 3 times as many as Bonnie, and Calvin gets 6 more than Alan. How many marbles does each person get?

Larry uses bags and dots in his diagram, but Serena says she has a simpler way to represent the problem. She uses the letter x and algebraic thinking.

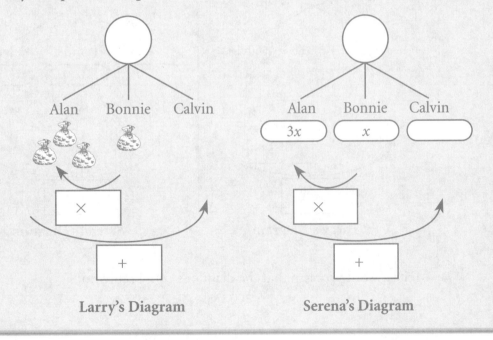

Larry's Diagram   Serena's Diagram

1. Complete each diagram above.

2. Serena writes an equation for her diagram. Complete her equation.

$$3x + x + \underline{\hspace{1.5cm}} = 153$$

③ Solve the equation in Item 2 and then complete each statement.

    a. Alan gets _____ marbles.

    b. Bonnie gets _____ marbles.

    c. Calvin gets _____ marbles.

④ Larry and Serena draw different diagrams for another problem about how Alan, Bonnie, and Calvin share some marbles. Complete each diagram.

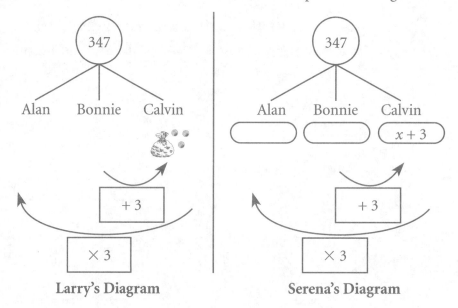

    Larry's Diagram   **Serena's Diagram**

⑤ Write a word problem that the diagrams could represent.

⑥ Write and then solve an equation for Serena's diagram.

(7) Now complete each statement.

    a. Alan gets _____ marbles.

    b. Bonnie gets _____ marbles.

    c. Calvin gets _____ marbles.

(8) Larry decides to use Serena's method to solve this problem. Complete Larry's diagram.

Petra, Solly, and Melrose have saved $285 altogether. Solly has saved 2 times as much as Petra, and Melrose has saved $53 more than Petra. How much has each person saved?

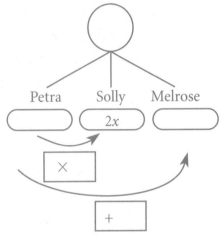

(9) Explain why Serena's algebraic method is a simpler way to represent this problem than drawing a diagram with bags and dots.

(10) Write and then solve an equation for Larry's completed diagram.

11 Complete the table, using your calculations from Item 10.

Name	Algebraic Value	Amount Saved ($)
Petra		
Solly	$2x$	
Melrose		

 12 Serena thinks that Larry also could have used either of the following diagrams to solve the same problem. Complete each diagram.

> Petra, Solly, and Melrose have saved $285 altogether. Solly has saved 2 times as much as Petra, and Melrose has saved $53 more than Petra. How much has each person saved?

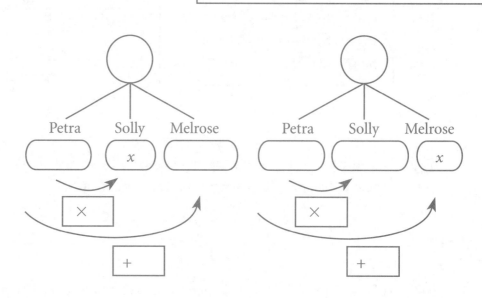

 13 Write and solve an equation for each diagram.

Complete each table below, using your calculations from Item 13.

Name	Algebraic Value	Amount Saved ($)
Petra		
Solly	x	
Melrose		

Name	Algebraic Value	Amount Saved ($)
Petra		
Solly		
Melrose	x	

 Serena says that any of the three diagrams in Items 8 and 12 will lead to the same solution. Decide whether she is correct. Explain your reasoning.

Alexis uses algebra to solve the following problem.

Petra, Solly, and Melrose have saved $333 altogether. Petra has saved $47 more than Melrose, and Melrose has saved $28 less than Solly. How much has each person saved?

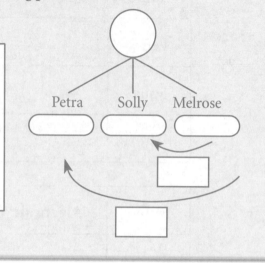

16 Complete the diagram and then write and solve an equation for the completed diagram.

17 Complete the table.

Name	Algebraic Value	Amount Saved ($)
Petra		
Solly		
Melrose		

18 Complete the diagram for this problem.

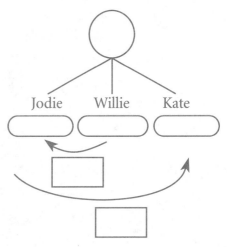

> Jodie, Willie, and Kate have saved $559 altogether. Jodie has saved $94 less than Willie. Kate has saved half as much as Jodie. How much has each person saved?

19 Write and solve an equation for the completed diagram.

20 Complete the table.

Name	Algebraic Value	Amount Saved ($)
Jodie		
Willie		
Kate		

21 Complete the diagram for this problem by writing three algebraic expressions and the total amount saved.

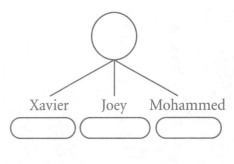

> Xavier, Joey, and Mohammed have saved $698 altogether. Mohammed has saved $86 more than Joey. Xavier has saved twice as much as Mohammed. How much has each person saved?

Write and solve an equation for the completed diagram in Item 21.

 Complete the table.

Name	Algebraic Value	Amount Saved ($)
Xavier		
Joey		
Mohammed		

 Complete the diagram for this problem, using algebra.

Marnie, Hillary, and Josiah buy gifts for Mother's Day. Hillary spends $28 less than Marnie. Marnie spends twice as much as Josiah. Altogether they spend $92. How much did each person spend?

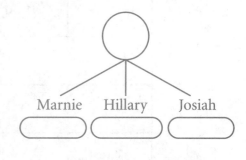

 Write and solve an equation for the completed diagram.

26 Now complete this table.

Name	Algebraic Value	Amount Saved ($)
Marnie		
Hillary		
Josiah		

Task C

Judy uses algebra to solve this problem.

Colenso Middle School has a total of 871 students in grades 7, 8, and 9. Grade 7 has 65 more students than Grade 8, and Grade 7 has $1\frac{1}{2}$ times as many students as Grade 9. How many students are in each grade?

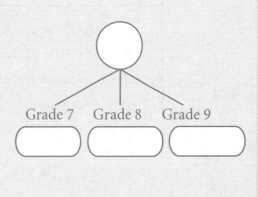

27 Complete the diagram. Then write and solve an equation for the completed diagram.

Now complete this table, using your calculations in Item 27.

Grade	Algebraic Value	Number of Students
7		
8		
9		

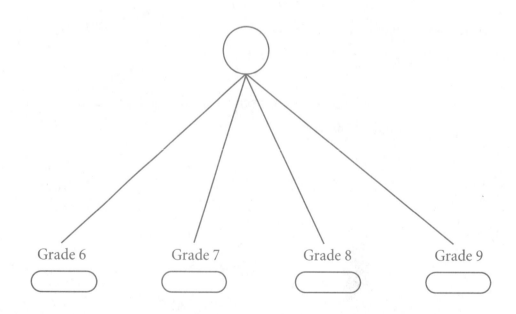 Christine challenges Dan to complete this diagram for the problem below, using algebra. Write the missing number in the circle and then write an algebraic expression in each oval.

Napier Middle School has a total of 1,003 students in grades 6 through 9. In Grade 6 there are 43 fewer students than in Grade 7. In Grade 9 there are 50 more students than in Grade 6, and in Grade 8 there are 20 fewer students than in Grade 9. How many students are there in each grade at the school?

Grade 6   Grade 7   Grade 8   Grade 9

Write and solve an equation for the completed diagram in Item 29.

 Now complete the table.

Grade	Algebraic Value	Number of Students
6		
7		
8		
9		

Page 49

Investigating Equation Pyramids

Task A

Janine has a rule for making equation pyramids. She calls it the A + B rule. The upside-down pyramid to the right shows how it works.

A		B
	A + B	

In each set of three boxes separated by a shaded box, the value in the lower box is the *sum* of the values in the two boxes above.

1. Write an algebraic expression in the empty space in the following equation pyramid, using Janine's A + B rule.

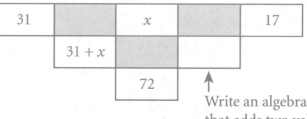

31		x		17
	31 + x			
		72	↑	

Write an algebraic expression that adds two values.

2. Janine writes an equation using the A + B rule and the two lower rows of the pyramid. She then simplifies the equation to get $2x + 48 = 72$. Show how Janine got this equation and then solve it for x.

3 Now check your calculations by substituting the value of x in each expression and writing the results in the empty boxes in the equation pyramid. (Hint: Be sure all the values follow the A + B rule.)

31				17
		72		

4 Complete each equation pyramid, using Janine's A + B rule to write the missing algebraic expressions. Write and solve the equation for each pyramid and show your work. (Hint: Check your solution by finding a numeric value for each box. Be sure all the values follow the rule.)

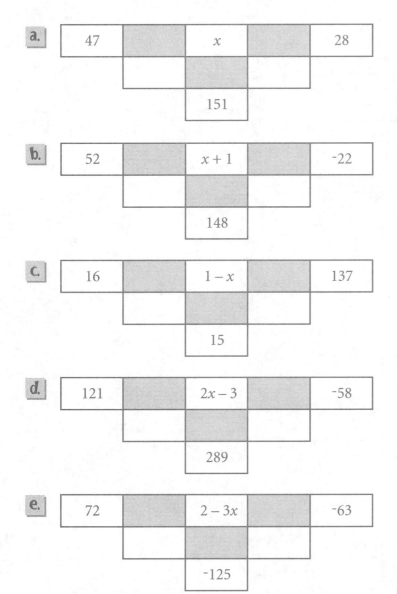

a.

47		x		28
		151		

b.

52		$x + 1$		-22
		148		

c.

16		$1 - x$		137
		15		

d.

121		$2x - 3$		-58
		289		

e.

72		$2 - 3x$		-63
		-125		

f.

-232		5x + 3		-17
		57		

5 Complete each equation pyramid, using Janine's A + B rule. Write and solve the equation for each pyramid. Show your work. Check your solution.

a.

x		4 + x		28
		360		

b.

4x + 1		2x − 9		⁻x + 4
		-41		

c.

9 − 5x		1 − x		237
		3		

d.

4x − 1		x − 32		-27
		10x		

e.

4x + 1		1 − 9x		⁻2x + 7
		⁻6x		

f.

⁻7 − 9x		3x + 8		⁻3x − 5
		x − 66		

Janine's friend Eugene creates a new rule for equation pyramids. He calls it the A + 2B rule.

A		B
	A + 2B	

 Complete the following equation pyramid, using Eugene's A + 2B rule.

8		x		5
	8 + 2x			
		96		

7 Eugene writes an equation for the pyramid, using his A + 2B rule for the two lower rows of the pyramid. He then simplifies the equation to get 28 + 4x = 96. Show how Eugene got this equation.

8 Solve the final equation. Show your work.

9 Now check your calculations by substituting the value of x in the expressions in Item 6 and writing the values in the empty boxes in the equation pyramid. Remember that all the values must follow the A + 2B rule.

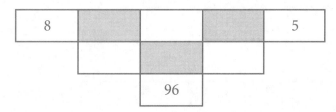

8				5
		96		

10 Complete each equation pyramid, using Eugene's A + 2B rule. Write and solve the equation for each pyramid and show your work. Check your solution.

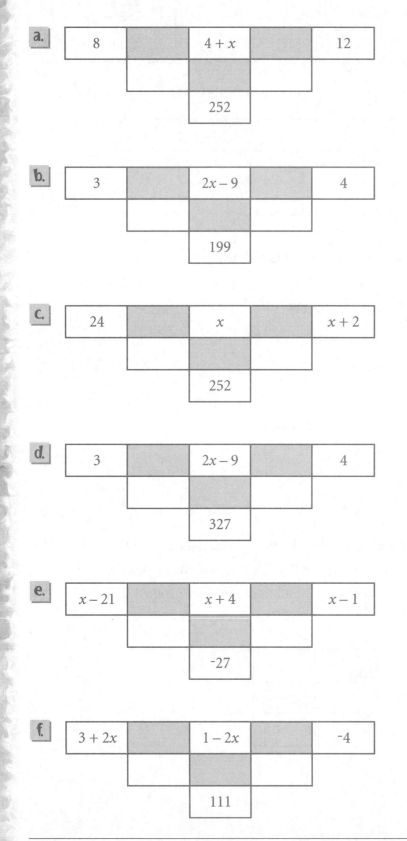

a.
8		4 + x		12
		252		

b.
3		2x − 9		4
		199		

c.
24		x		x + 2
		252		

d.
3		2x − 9		4
		327		

e.
x − 21		x + 4		x − 1
		-27		

f.
3 + 2x		1 − 2x		-4
		111		

Algebra Makes Sense

Complete each equation pyramid, using Eugene's A + 2B rule. Write and solve each pyramid equation and show your work. Check your solution.

a.

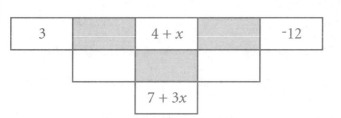

| 3 | | 4 + x | | -12 |

| | 7 + 3x | |

b.

| -3 | | 2x − 3 | | 4 |

| | 10x | |

c.

| x | | 4 − x | | -3 |

| | x − 42 | |

d.

| -5 | | x + 5 | | x − 1 |

| | -3x | |

e.

| x + 9 | | 1 − 2x | | x − 3 |

| | 6x − 5 | |

f.

| -5 − 3x | | 1 − 2x | | x + 5 |

| | x + 3 | |

Eugene's friend Megan decides to make her own rule, which she calls the A – B rule.

A		B
	A – B	

 Complete the following equation pyramid, using Megan's A – B rule.

6		x		2
	6 – x			
		-24		

 Megan writes an equation for the pyramid, using her A – B rule for the two lower rows of the pyramid. She then simplifies the equation to get $8 - 2x = -24$. Show how Megan got this equation.

Solve Megan's equation and show your work.

Now check your calculations by substituting the value of x in the expressions in Item 12 and writing the values in the empty boxes in the equation pyramid. Be sure the values you have written follow the A – B rule.

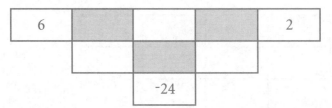

Complete each equation pyramid, using Megan's A – B rule. Write and solve the equation for each pyramid and show your work. Check your solution.

a.

8		x		10

	8	

b.

16		x – 9		3

	-37	

c.

25		2x		x + 13

	77	

d.

9 + 3x		3 – 2x		4x

	157	

e.

14		-2x		3x + 1

	3x – 1	

f.

9 – 3x		4 – x		2x + 1

	-5 – 6x	

Ellen wrote a new rule for an equation pyramid. Ellen's rule uses multiplication and subtraction.

A			B
	A − 2B		

17 Complete each equation pyramid, using this A − 2B rule. Write and solve the equation for each pyramid and show your work. Check your solution.

a.

4		x		7
		4		

b.

27		$2x − 7$		x
		x		

c.

$3x − 6$		$2x − 1$		$x + 4$
		77		

d.

$9 + 3x$		$3 − 2x$		$4x$
		$x − 55$		

e.

$3 − 5x$		$3x − 2$		$x + 7$
		0		

f.

1 + 3x		3 − 4x		4x − 1
		30x		

18 Find the rule for each equation pyramid below. Write the rule in the empty box beside the pyramid. (Hint: You may need to use more than one operation.) Write and solve the equation for each pyramid in the space below the pyramid.

a.

2		x		-6
	4 − x		2x + 6	
		-24		

A		B

↑
Write the rule here.

b.

3		x		-1
	6 + 3x		2x − 3	
		3x − 6		

A		B

↑
Write the rule here.

Practice PLUS 3

Page 50

Investigating Arithmagons and Other Problems

 **Task A**

The sum of any pair of circle numbers in an *arithmagon* must equal the number in the box between them.

Arnie thinks that he can use algebra to find the missing circle numbers in this arithmagon. He begins by writing x in one circle. Then he writes another expression in each of the other circles.

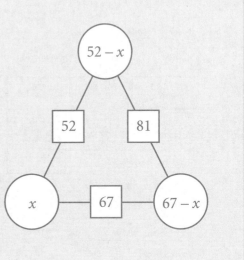

1. Explain why Arnie writes $52 - x$ in one circle and $67 - x$ in the other circle.

2. Now write an equation relating these two circles and solve it to find the value for x in the arithmagon. (Hint: Use the box number 81 in your equation.)

Algebra Makes Sense

3 Use the value of x from Item 2 to write the missing circle numbers in Arnie's arithmagon. Check that they are correct by adding pairs of circle numbers and comparing each sum to the box value between them.

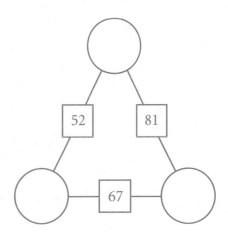

4 Write algebraic expressions for the missing circle numbers in each arithmagon on the left. Then write and solve an equation to find the value of x. Show your work. Write the missing circle numbers in each arithmagon on the right and check that they are correct.

a.

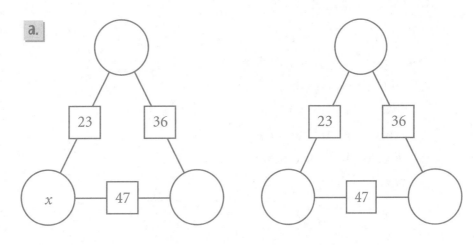

b.

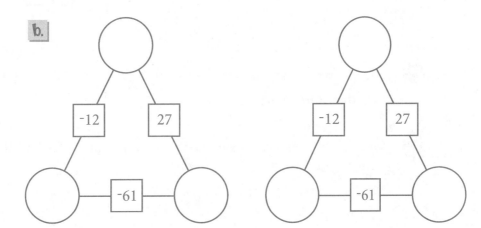

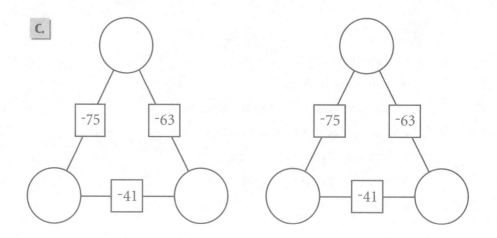

Task B

Julio thinks he can use Arnie's algebraic method to find the missing circle numbers for this pentagonal (5-sided) arithmagon. He begins by putting x in one circle.

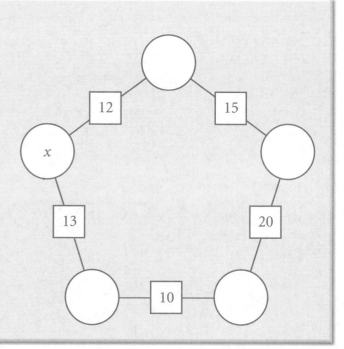

5. Use x to write algebraic expressions that represent the missing numbers in the other four circles.

6. Write and then solve an equation to find the value of x for Julio's arithmagon.

7 Write the missing circle numbers in the arithmagon below. Check that the circle values are correct by adding pairs of circle values and comparing each sum to the box value between them.

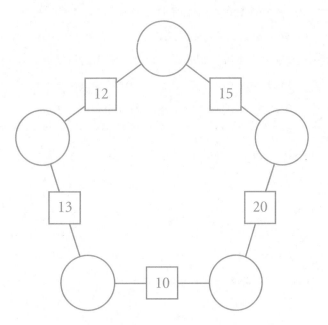

8 Write algebraic expressions for the missing circle numbers in the arithmagon on the left. Then write and solve an equation for the arithmagon. Show your work. Write the missing circle numbers in the arithmagon on the right and check that they are correct.

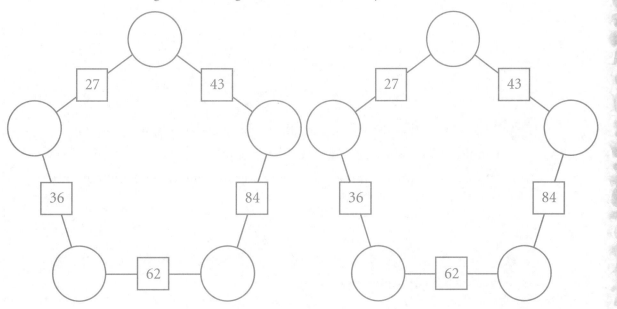

Joni looks at these three sums of two consecutive numbers and concludes that the sum of any two consecutive numbers is an odd number. Joni uses algebra to see if this is always true. She begins by using *n* to stand for any number. She writes the sum of any two consecutive numbers as $n + (n + 1)$.

$$19 + 20 = 39$$
$$28 + 29 = 57$$
$$37 + 38 = 75$$

 What does $n + 1$ represent?

 Joni simplifies $n + (n + 1)$ to get $2n + 1$. She then says that since $2n + 1$ is always odd, the sum of any two consecutive numbers is always odd. Is she correct? Explain why or why not.

 What two consecutive numbers can be added to give 3,139? Show your work.

 Joni thinks that the sum of any three consecutive numbers is also a multiple of 3. Write an algebraic expression to represent the sum of any three consecutive numbers. Use the letter *n* to stand for the first number.

13 Simplify your expression from Item 12. Then use it to explain why Joni is correct. Show your work.

Algebra Makes Sense

The sum of three consecutive numbers is 444. Use algebra to find the three numbers.

 Show that the sum of any four consecutive numbers is $4n + 6$ when n stands for the first number.

 Joni's friend Marg says that because the sum of any three consecutive numbers is a multiple of 3, then the sum of any four consecutive numbers is a multiple of 4. Use your work from Item 15 to help explain why Marg is incorrect.

 The sum of four consecutive numbers is 1,082. Use algebra to find the four numbers.

Page 51

During rush hour, 16,000 cars per hour use the freeway going from Compton toward Los Angeles. The number of vehicles entering the freeway at City Heights is 20% of the number already on the freeway from Compton. The number of vehicles entering from the access ramp at the airport is 2,000 more than the number entering from City Heights.

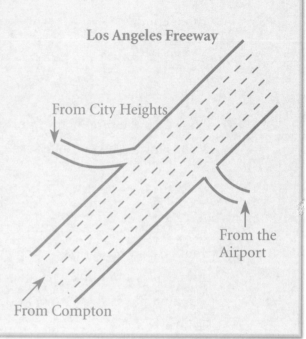

Los Angeles Freeway

From City Heights

From the Airport

From Compton

18. Write an equation that describes the traffic flow for this situation.

19. Solve the equation and then calculate the number of vehicles that have entered the freeway from each route.

 a. Number of cars from Compton = _____

b. Number of cars from City Heights = _____

c. Number of cars from the airport = _____

Mark is 3 times as old as his son, Gerry. The sum of their ages is 52 years. You can use algebra to find their ages.

Write an equation representing this situation.

 Solve the equation and find the ages of Mark and Gerry.

 Solve each problem, using algebra.

 Mary is 27 years younger than her mom, Ellie. Their combined ages total 73. Calculate the ages of Mary and Ellie.

 In 12 years, Bill will be twice as old as his daughter, Connie, and their combined ages will total 72 years. Calculate how old Bill and Connie are now.

 Wyatt is 32 years older than his son, Al. Ten years ago he was 3 times as old as Al was then. Calculate their present ages.

Practice PLUS 1

1 Complete this diagram for Alan, Bonnie, and Calvin.

Alan, Bonnie, and Calvin share
518 marbles. Bonnie receives
2 less than Calvin, and Alan gets
3 times as many as Calvin.

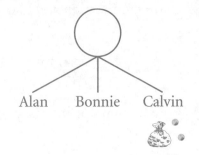

Alan   Bonnie   Calvin

2 Now complete the table. Show your calculations.

Name	Number of Marbles
Alan	
Bonnie	
Calvin	

Algebra Makes Sense

Complete the diagram for this problem, using algebra.

Doris, Julian, and Grayson share a prize for $571. Doris receives 4 times as much as Julian. Julian receives $47 more than Grayson. How much money does each person get?

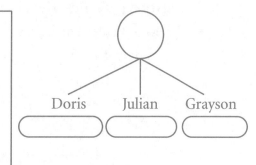

Doris   Julian   Grayson

 Write and solve an equation for the completed diagram.

 Complete the table.

Name	Algebraic Value	Share of the Prize($)
Doris		
Julian		
Grayson		

1. Jerry has a rule for making equation pyramids. He calls it the 2A – B rule. The figure shows how it works.

A		B
	2A – B	

a. Fill in the empty box in the following equation pyramid, using Jerry's 2A – B rule.

31		x		6 – x
	62 – x			
		80		

b. Jerry writes the equation $124 - 2x - 3x + 6 = 80$. Show how Jerry got this equation. Then simplify the equation and solve it.

c. Now check your calculations by writing the values in the empty boxes in the equation pyramid. Be sure your values follow Jerry's rule.

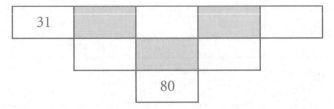

31				
		80		

Algebra Makes Sense

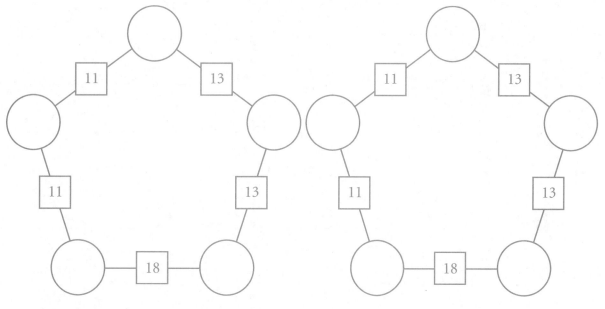

1 The sum of any pair of circle numbers gives the value of the number in the box between them.

 a. Use *x* to write algebraic expressions for the missing circle numbers in the arithmagon on the left above. Then write and solve an equation to find the value of *x*. Show your work below.

 b. Now write the circle numbers you have found in the matching arithmagon on the right above and check your answers.

2 If the first number in a sequence of 5 consecutive numbers is *n*, the five numbers are *n*, *n* + 1, *n* + 2, *n* + 3, and *n* + 4. Explain why the sum of any five consecutive numbers is a multiple of 5.

1 Complete the following sequences.

a. 6, 11, 16, _____, _____, _____, _____, _____, _____

b. 100, 40, ⁻20, _____, _____, _____, _____, _____, _____

c. 15, 24, _____, 42, _____, 60, _____, _____, _____, _____

d. _____, _____, _____, 10, 17, 24, _____, _____, _____

e. _____, _____, ⁻$15\frac{1}{2}$, ⁻11, ⁻$6\frac{1}{2}$, _____, _____, _____, _____

f. _____, _____, _____, ⁻24.7, ⁻22.6, ⁻20.5, _____, _____, _____

2 Write the values that go in cells B7 through B13 in each spreadsheet. Then write the function for each, showing that *y* dollars are saved after *x* weeks.

a.

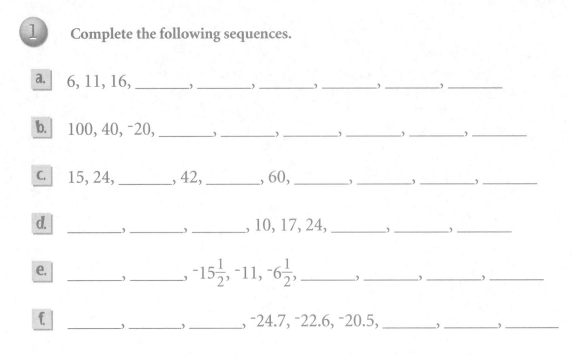

	A	B	C
	Week	Savings ($)	
1			
2	0	50	
3	1	62	
4	2	74	
5	3	86	
6	4	98	
7	5		
8	6		
9	7		
10	8		
11	9		
12	10		
13	11		

Kirby's Savings Record (SS) — A14

b.

	A	B	C
	Week	Savings ($)	
1			
2	0	12.50	
3	1	20.50	
4	2	28.50	
5	3	36.50	
6	4	44.50	
7	5		
8	6		
9	7		
10	8		
11	9		
12	10		
13	11		

Barb's Savings Record (SS) — B7

y = _____

y = _____

Samantha's Plumbing has special weekend rates.

Samantha's Plumbing
$80 weekend fee plus $55 per hour

a. Complete the boxes in the following flowchart showing how the hours worked and the total charge are related.

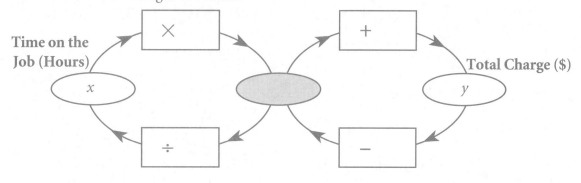

b. Samantha's Plumbing charges y dollars for x hours of weekend repair work. Complete each function, using the flowchart to help you.

$y =$ _____ $x =$ _____

c. Use the functions from Exercise 3b to calculate the missing values in each table.

Number of Hours (x)	Total Dollars Charged (y)
2	
	327.50
0.25	

Number of Hours (x)	Total Dollars Charged (y)
	245.00
	382.50
7	

4 Solve each equation. Show your work.

a. $28 + 4x = 94 + x$

b. $16 + 6x = 76 + 2x$

c. $13 - 2x = {}^-97 - 12x$

d. $44 - 3x = 43 - 2x$

5 Simplify the expressions in each table.

a.

Expression	Simplified Expression
$8w - 10 + 8w - 14$	
$24 - 7r - 14 + 17r$	
$^-19 - 12x + 21 + 12x$	
$^-39t + 17 - t + 30t$	

b.

Expression	Simplified Expression
$4w + 9 + 10s - 14w$	
$120 - 8r - 130 + 2s$	
$^-20p - 18x + 78 + 18x$	
$^-8q - 3 + 43d + 138q$	

 6 Expand and then simplify the expressions in each table.

a.

Expression	Expanded	Simplified
$6(2x - 1) + 2(2x - 8)$		
$3(m - 4) + 3(2m - 1)$		
$2(8 - s) + 3(s - 8)$		
$3(1 - 3y) + 9(1 - y)$		

b.

Expression	Expanded	Simplified
$10(2a - 7) - 5(3a + 1)$		
$3(4x - 4) - 6(2x - 5)$		
$^-2(6 - 3x) - 5(1 - 3x)$		
$^-5(1 - 3y) - 10(5 - 2y)$		